AF260839

Landscape Touch
Vol. 5

Sun Mi Kwon

ABOUT THIS BOOK

Welcome to a visual journey designed to inspire outdoor living possibilities. This book is crafted with the vision of empowering new homeowners to curate outdoor spaces that resonate with their lifestyle, while offering contractors and architects fresh perspectives and innovative ideas to elevate their craft, portfolios, and businesses. It serves as a valuable educational resource for students striving for excellence in their projects. With stunning and distinctive night views illuminated by captivating lighting designs, this book stands out as a unique treasure in its genre. Join us now as we explore the realm of endless possibilities. May this book guide you towards achieving your desired outdoor oasis. Whether you choose to implement the entire design or incorporate select elements, you'll find endless inspiration to enhance your outdoor living experience.

TABLE OF CONTENTS

House 5 - Day View

House 5 - Night View

Day View

2D FLOOR PLAN VIEW

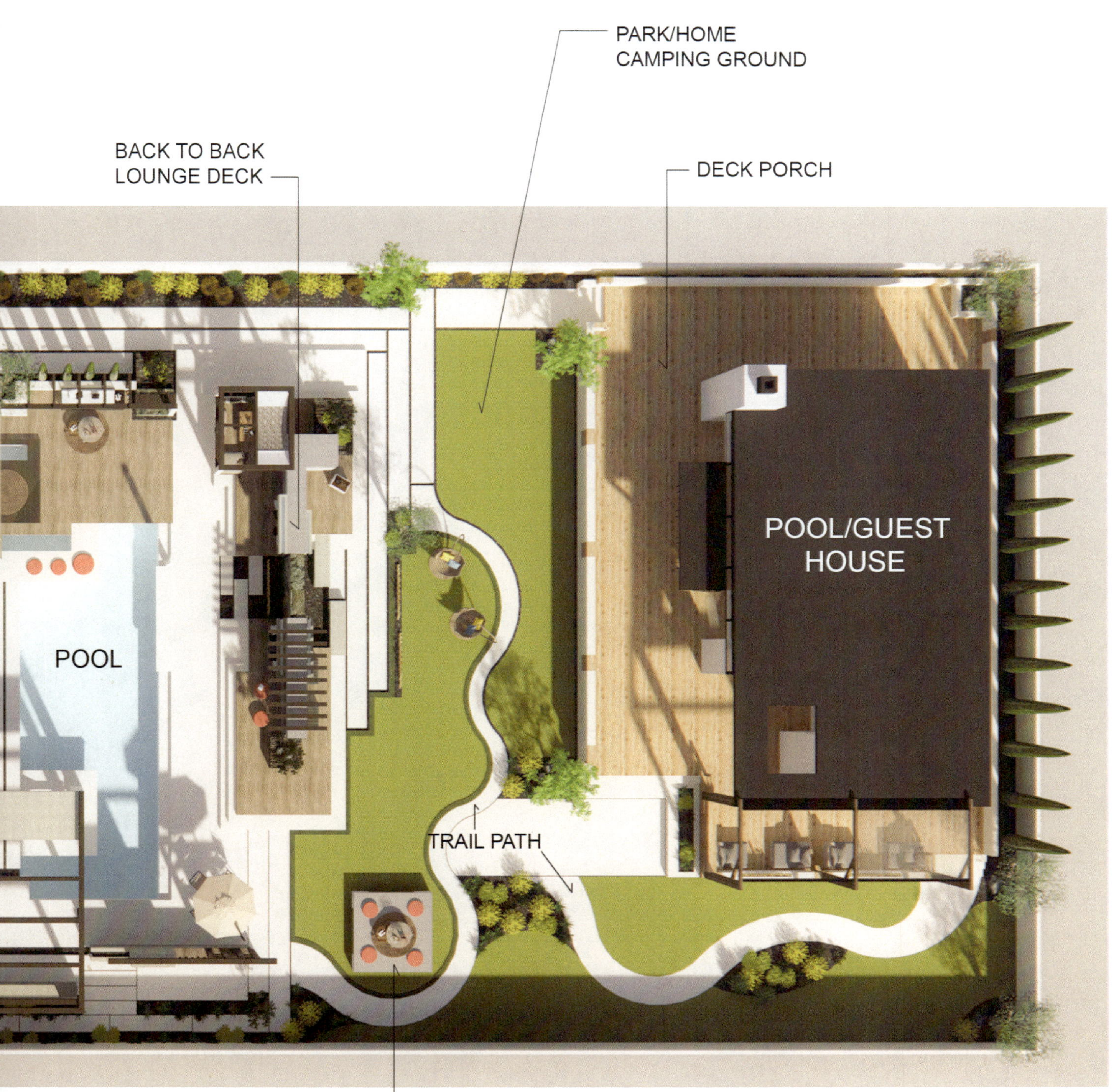
PARK/HOME
CAMPING GROUND
BACK TO BACK
LOUNGE DECK
DECK PORCH
POOL/GUEST
HOUSE
POOL
TRAIL PATH
OPEN LOUNGE

3D HOUSE VIEW 1

BACK TO BACK RAISED DECK LOUNGE
(POOL & PARK SIDE)
GREEN PARK/HOME CAMP GROUND
POOL/GUEST
HOUSE
BENCH DECK W/ACCENT FIRE PIT

3D HOUSE VIEW 2

HOUSE FRONT ISO VIEW

HOUSE RIGHT ISO VIEW

HOUSE MAIN ENTRY VIEW W/WROUGHT IRON GATE & FENCE

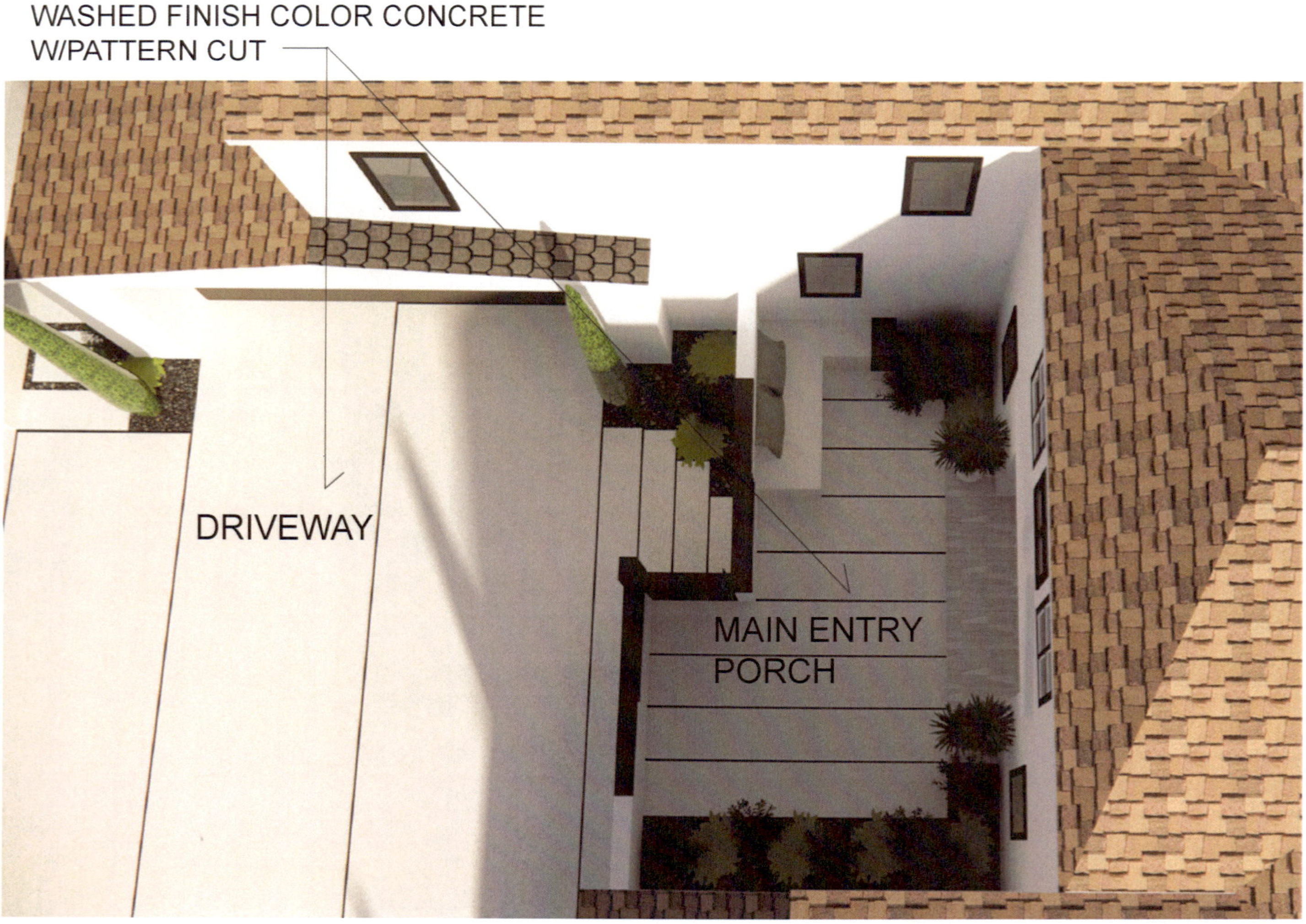

WASHED FINISH COLOR CONCRETE
W/PATTERN CUT

DRIVEWAY

MAIN ENTRY
PORCH

GARAGE VIEW

WALKWAY TO SIDE YARD
& DRIVEWAY
DRIVEWAY

WALKWAY TO RIGHT
SIDE YARD
W/LOW SEATING
WALL

RIGHT SIDE YARD WALKWAY
W/ACCENT BENCH
(SMOOTH STUCCO FINISH)

CALIFORNIA ROOM 1
W/LOUNGE FURNITURES

BBQ
&
DINING
AREA

CALIFORNIA ROOM 1
W/FLOOR FIRE PIT

BACKYARD VIEW FROM **CALIFORNIA ROOM 1**

SPA & DECK

WALKWAYS W/PLANTER

CALIFORNIA ROOM 1

CALIFORNIA ROOM 2

CALIFORNIA ROOM 2

ACCESS WALKWAY W/PLANTERS

CALIFORNIA ROOM 2 INTERIOR VIEW W/ACCESS TO CALIFORNIA ROOM 1

WASHED FINISH COLOR CONCRETE
W/DECORATIVE TILE BANDS

FLOOR FIRE PIT

DAY BED LOUNGE FACING CALIFORNIA ROOM 2

WROUGHT IRON FENCE

DAY BED W/SMOOTH STUCCO FINISH

DAY BED LOUNGE

SPA AREA OVER VIEW

POOL & SPA OPEN LOUNGE
W/FLOOR FIRE PIT

OPEN LOUNGE W/ FLOOR
FIRE PIT

SPA & LOUNGE OVER VIEW

SPA

RAISED
DECK
LOUNGE

SPA COPING DECK & SEATING VIEWS

POOL DECK LOUNGE W/OPEN PATIO COVER

ACCENT WATER ELEMENT W/1/2" POOL RETURN LINE
CANTILEVER POOL CABANA W/BAJA LOUNGE & FIRE PIT

POOL DECK LOUNGE W/SEATING BENCH &
OPEN PATIO COVER

BACK ACCESS **WALKWAY**

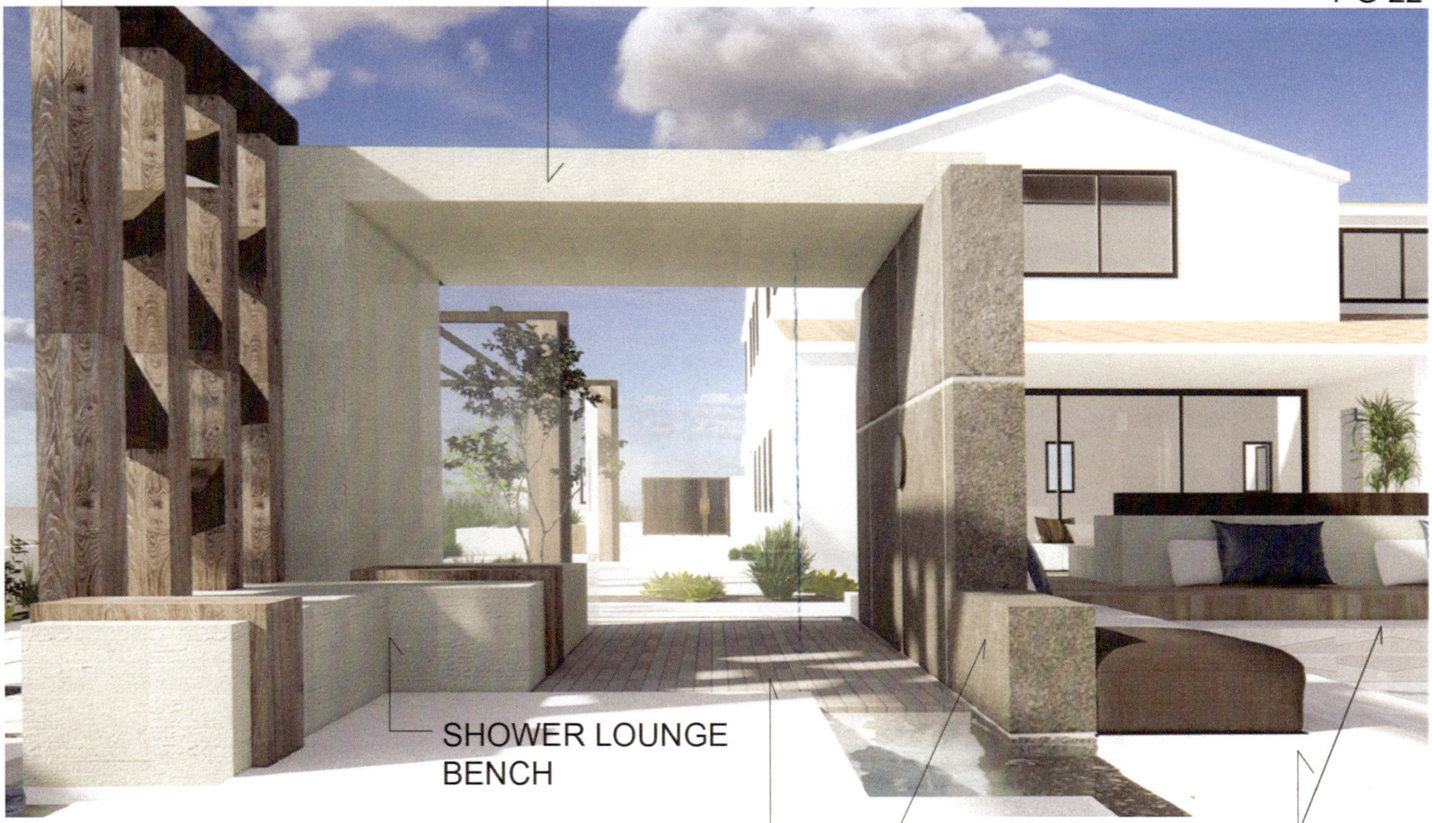
WOOD FRAME ACCENT PANEL
SMOOTH STUCCO FINISH
SHOWER LOUNGE BENCH
PORCELAIN OR COMPOSITE DECKING W/FLOOR DRAIN
NATURAL STONE OR OVERSIZED PORCELAIN TILE
SPA COPING DECK LOUNGE

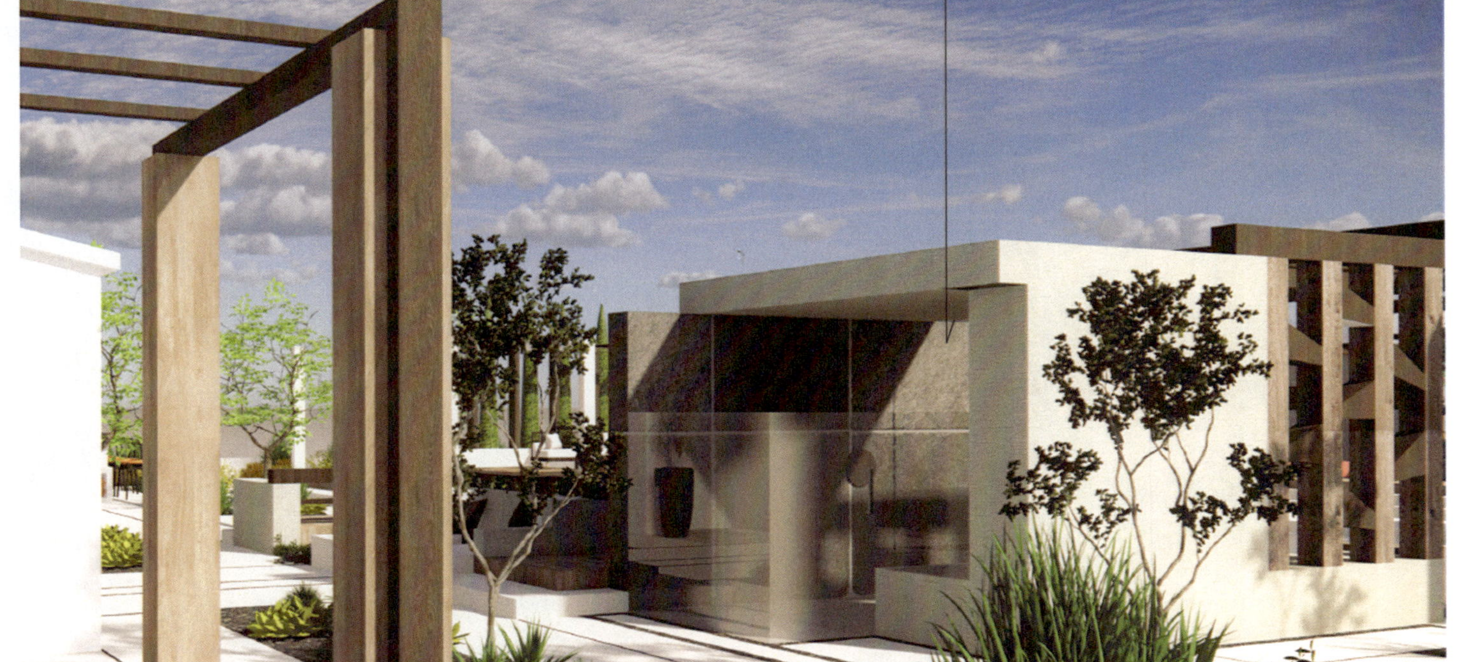

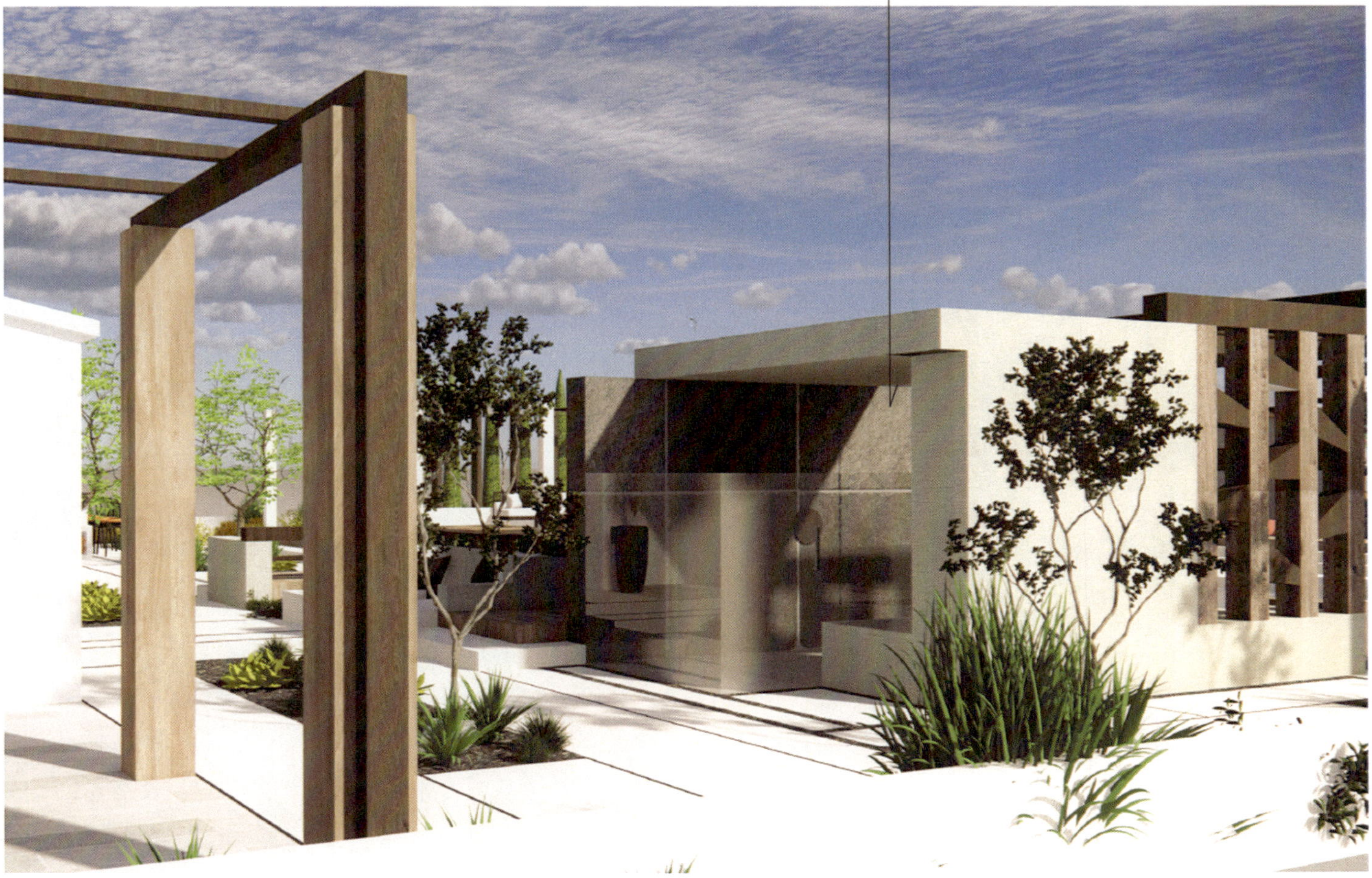

OUTDOOR SHOWER

BACK ACCESS WALKWAY VIEW FROM RIGHT SIDE YARD
OPEN PATIO COVER LOUNGE

OUTDOOR SHOWER
DAY BED
WALKWAY TO SIDE YARD
FLOOR FIRE PIT

CANTILEVER POOL CABANA W/BAJA LOUNGE & FIRE PIT

OPEN POOL DECK W/UMBRELLA TABLE SET

CANTILEVER POOL CABANA

CANTILEVER POOL CABANA W/BAJA LOUNGE

BACK TO BACK **RAISED LOUNGE DECK** W/FIRE PIT
(POOL SIDE)

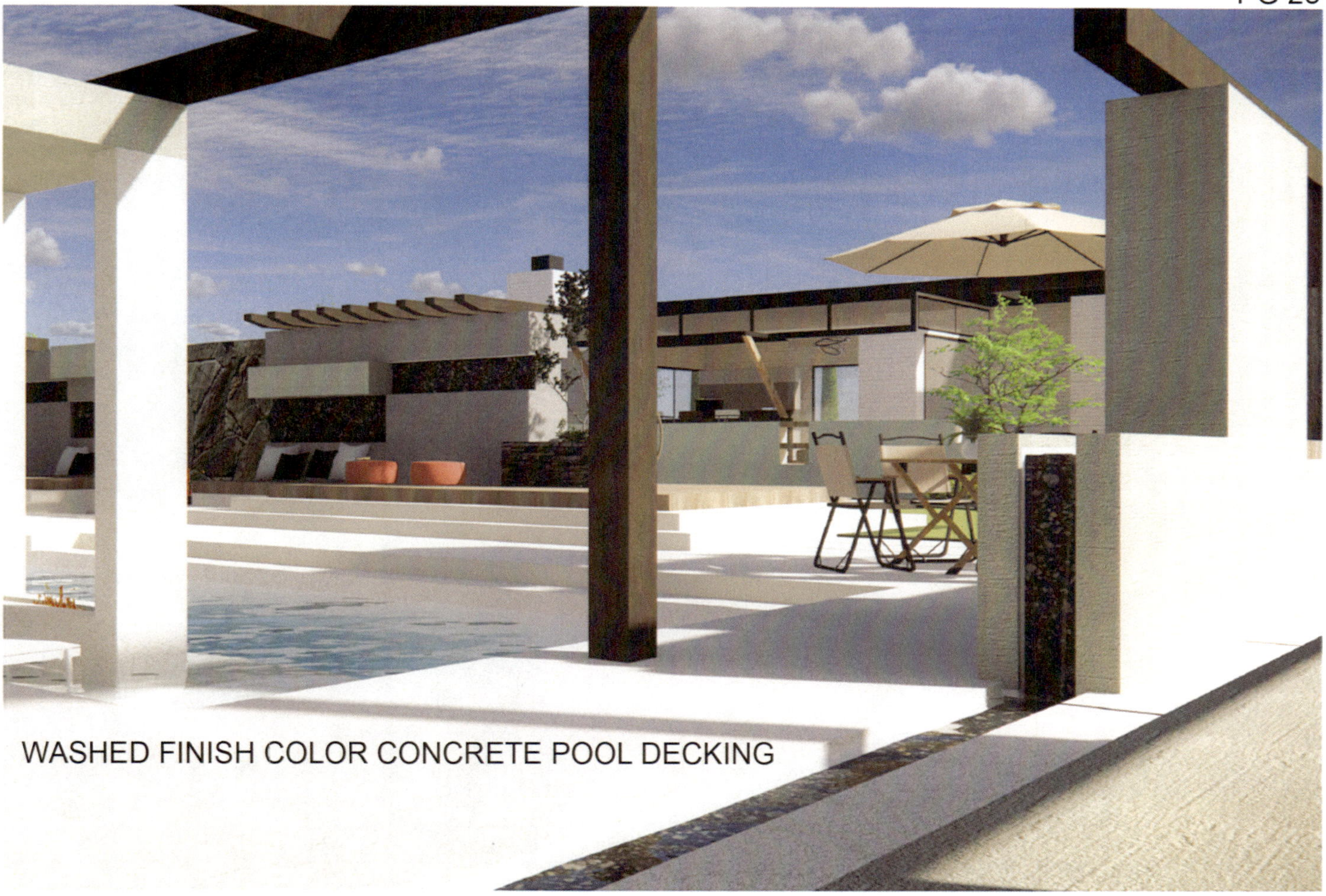
WASHED FINISH COLOR CONCRETE POOL DECKING

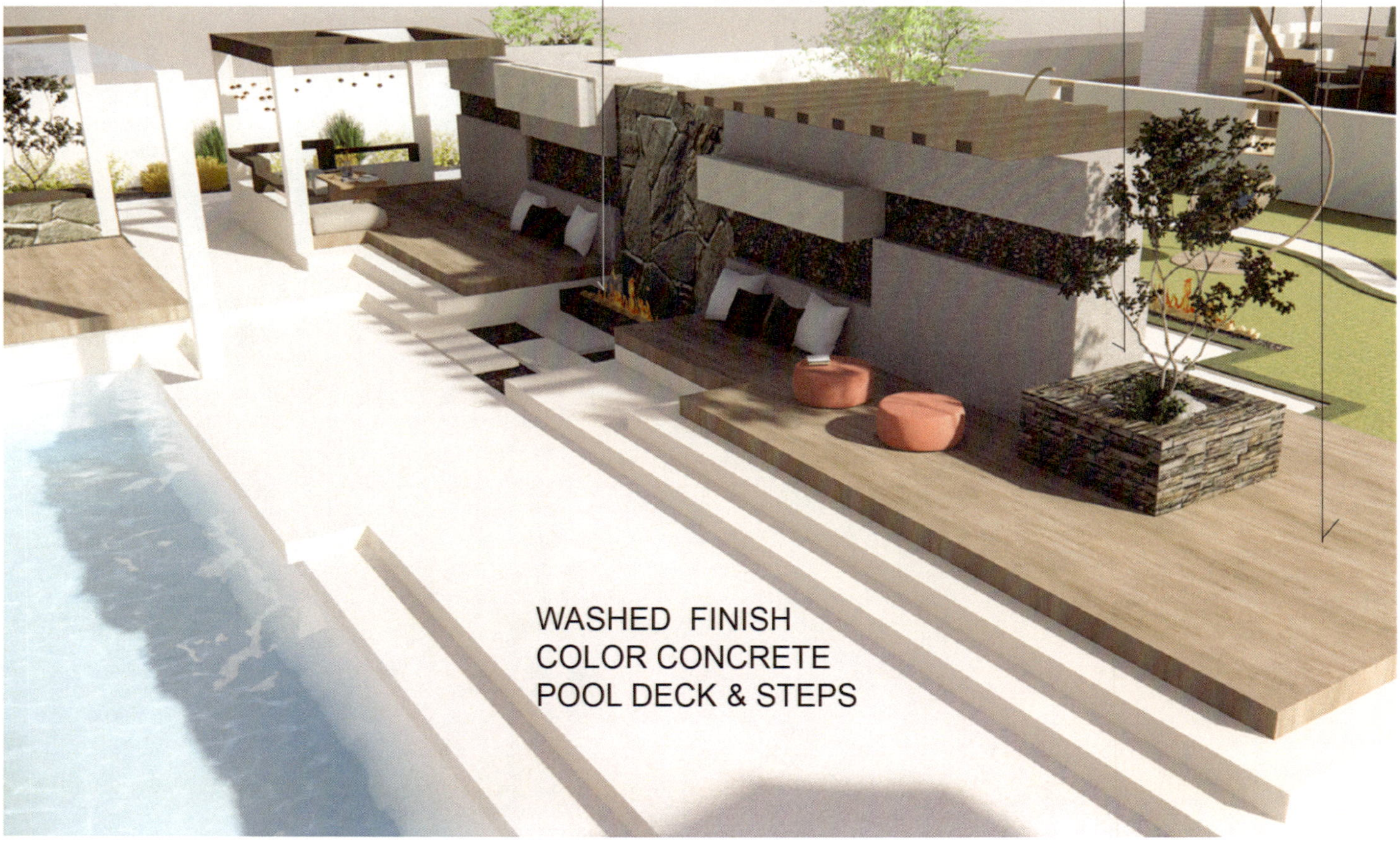
PORCELAIN TILE DECK
FIRE PIT
SMOOTH STUCCO FINISH
WASHED FINISH COLOR CONCRETE POOL DECK & STEPS

POOL SIDE RAISED LOUNGE DECK W/FIRE PIT & WATERFALL FEATURE

CASCADING WATERFALL W/NATURAL STONE VENEER
(7% WALL ANGLE W/UNDERGROUND WATER CATCH BASIN)

OPEN PATIO COVER RAISED DECK W/CANOPY SHADE

NATURAL STONE OR MANUFACTURAL STONE VENEER

POOL RAISED DECK LOUNGE

WASHED FINISH CONCRETE

FOOT SPA LOUNGE OVER VIEW

ACCENT TRELLIS

PORCELAIN TILE DECK W/2 TONE COLOR

POOL

16" SOLID CONCRETE SUNSHADE COLUMN

FOOT SPA SEATING LAYOUT

FOOT SPA & SEATING

BACK TO BACK RAISED DECK LOUNGE AREA OVER VIEW

WALKWAY
GREEN PARK & HOME CAMPING
BACK TO BACK RAISED LOUNGE DECK
W/FIRE PIT ON BOTH SIDE

BACK TO BACK RAISED LOUNGE DECK W/FIRE PIT & WATERFALL
FEATURE AT GREEN PARK SIDE

POOL/GUEST HOUSE VIEW W/GREEN PARK

GREEN PARK/HOME CAMPING GROUND OVER VIEW

BACK TO BACK RAISED DECK LOUNGE

W/FIRE PIT & WATERFALL FEATURE

FLOOR FIRE PIT

GREEN PARK/HOME CAMPING GROUND

NATURAL STONE VENEER/7% WALL ANGLE W/UNDERGROUND
WATER CATCH BASIN

SMOOTH STUCCO FINISH
WALL ACCENT RECESSED W/MOSAIC TILE
WORLD FAMOUS BRAND
POP FASHION
INSTITUTIONS OF
OUR DREAM AND HOPE
NATURAL STACKED STONE VENEER PLANTER BOX

POOL/GUEST HOUSE PORCH W/FIXED AWNING AT OUTDOOR BAR COUNTER

POOL/GUEST HOUSE PORCH DECK

POOL/GUEST HOUSE

STEEL FRAME PATIO COVER W/OPTIONAL AUTO RETRACTABLE
AWNING ON TOP FOR SHADE
GREEN PARK W/WALKWAYS

SIDE YARD OPEN PATIO LOUNGE
W/OPTIONAL WATER FEATURE
AT PLANTER

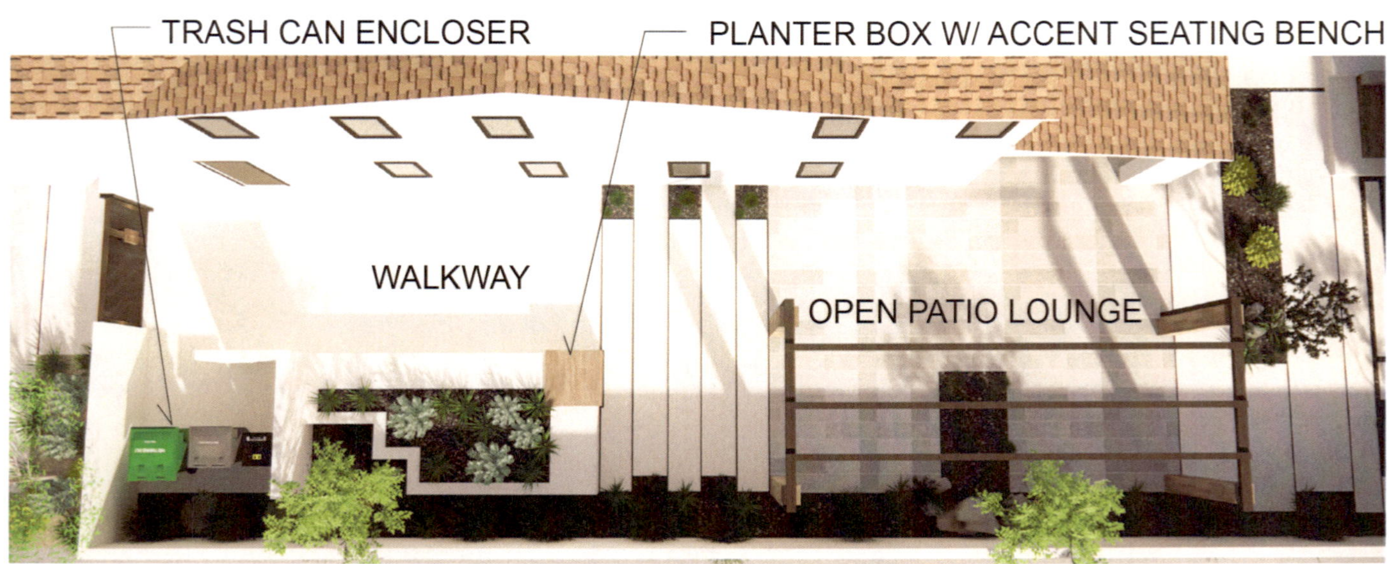

RIGHT SIDE YARD VIEW W/OPEN PATIO COVER LOUNGE

Night View

2D FLOOR PLAN VIEW

GREEN PARK/HOME CAMPING GROUND
FOOT SPA
WALKWAY
DECK PORCH
POOL/GUEST HOUSE
POOL
POOL CABANA
BACK TO BACK RAISED DECK
TRAIL PATH

HOUSE RIGHT ISO NIGHT VIEW

HOUSE FRONT ISO NIGHT VIEW 2

HOUSE LEFT ISO NIGHT VIEW 3

HOUSE MAIN ENTRY & GARAGE VIEW

HOUSE MAIN ENTRY WROUGHT IRON FENCE & GATE

TOP VIEW OF **MAIN HOUSE ENTRY PORCH**

FRONT RIGHT SIDEYARD ENTRY

6' DOUBLE GATE
& SMOOTH STUCCO FINISH WALL

FRONT LEFT SIDE
WALKWAY
TO LEFT SIDEYARD

LEFT SIDE GATE

WALKWAY

LEFT SIDE YARD

CALIFORNIA ROOM 1 W/FLOOR FIRE PIT

FLOOR FIRE PIT AT CALIFORNIA ROOM 1

WASHED FINISH COLOR CONCRETE
W/PATTERN CUT

WALKWAY

VIEW FROM **CALIFORNIA ROOM 1**

BBQ & DINING LAYOUT

NIGHT BED LOUNGE FACING CALIFORNIA ROOM 2

CALIFORNIA ROOM 2 W/FIRE PIT

VIEWS FROM **CALIFORNIA ROOM 2**

CALIFORNIA ROOM 2

CALIFORNIA ROOM 1
WASHED FINISH COLOR CONCRETE W/ACCENT TILE BANDS

OPEN PATIO LOUNGE
W/PLANTER

TRASH
ENCLOSER
PLANTER
BOX W/
SEATING
BENCH
GATE

RIGHT SIDE YARD
W/OPEN PATIO COVER
LOUNGE

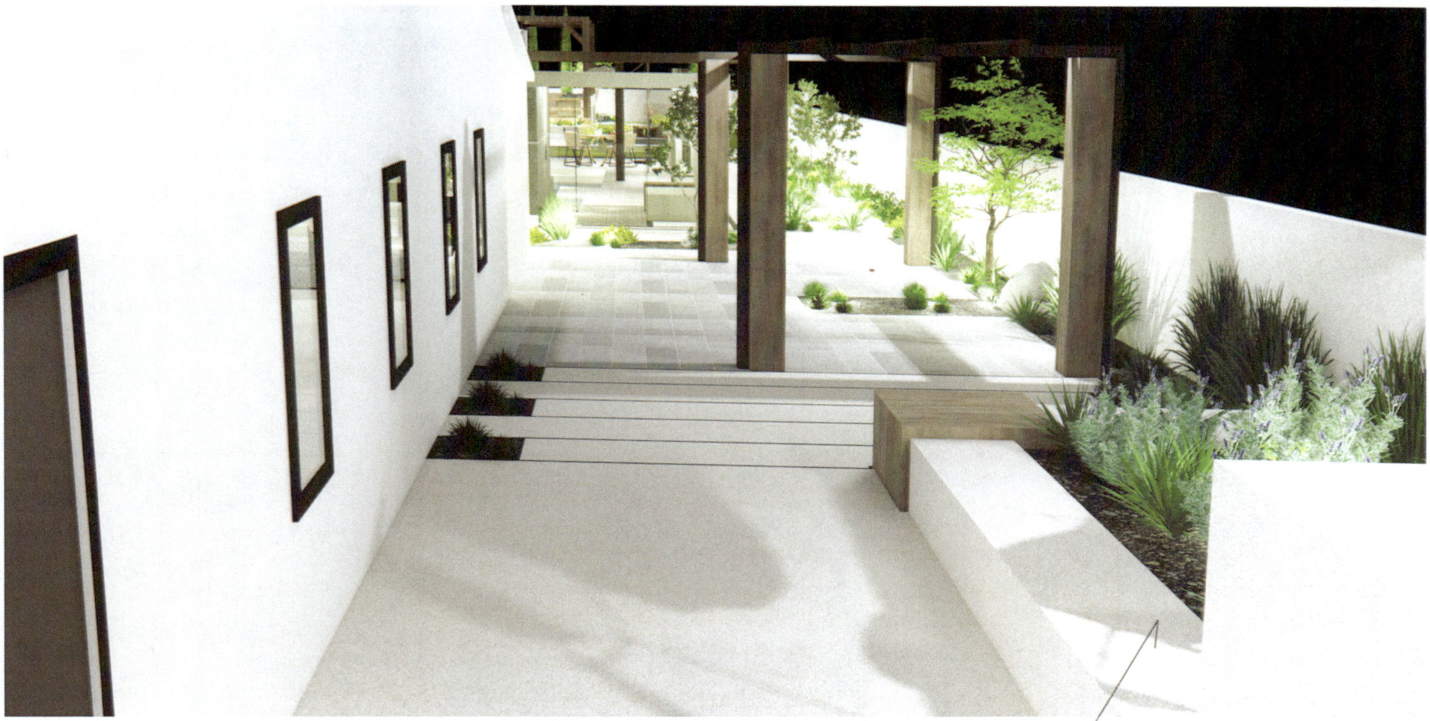

PLANTER BOX W/ ACCENT SEATING BENCH

RIGHT SIDE YARD

RIGHT SIDE YARD TO BACKYARD

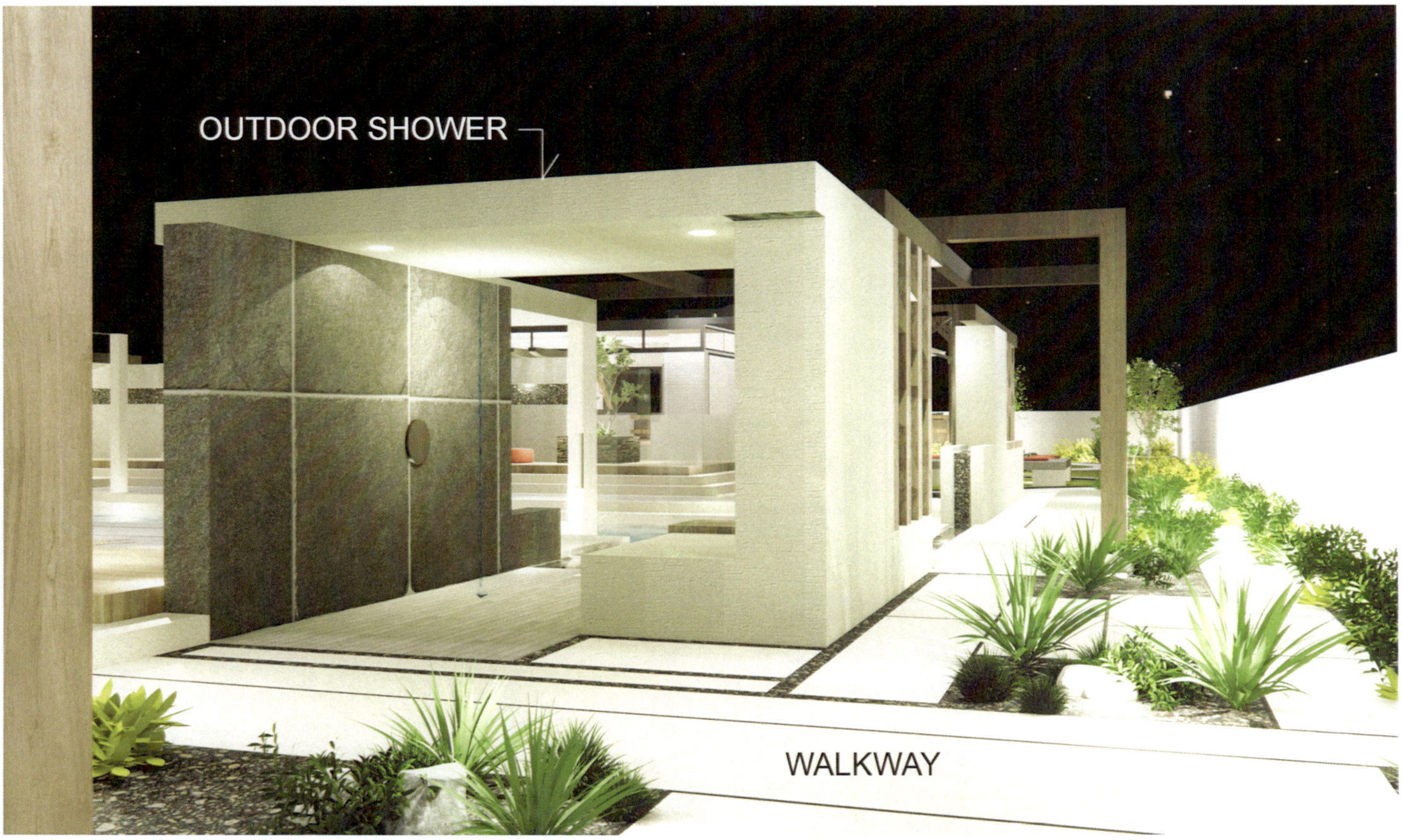

RIGHT SIDE HOUSE BACKYARD OVER VIEW

SPA & LOUNGE OVER VIEW

SPA W/COPING DECK LOUNGE

FLOOR FIRE PIT AT SPA LOUNGE

SPA & DECK LOUNGE
PORCELAIN TILE FINISH AT SPA COPING & DECK

CALIFORNIA ROOM 2

POOL & SPA LOUNGE OVER VIEW

CANTILEVER POOL CABANA

POOL BAJA LOUNGE AREA

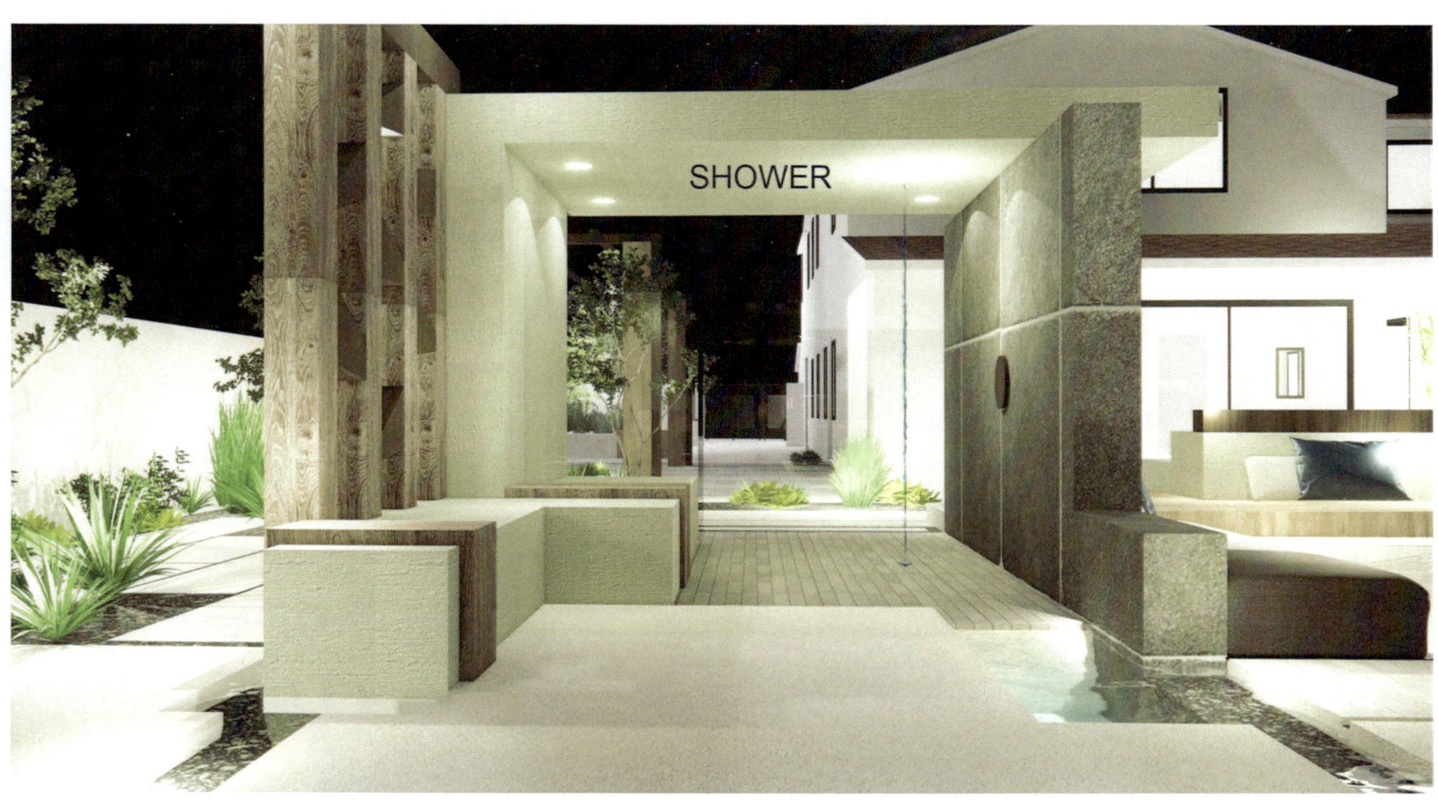

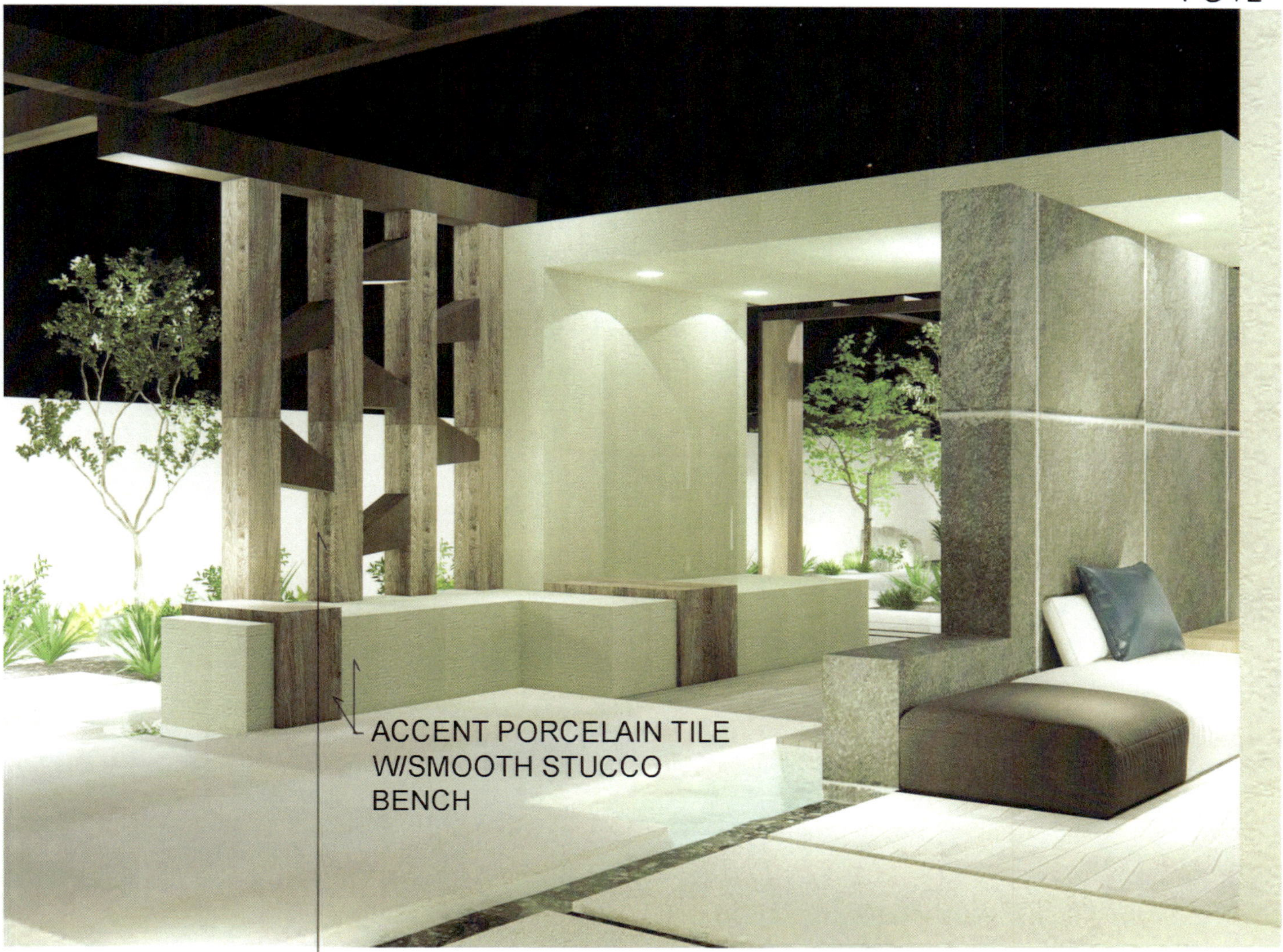
ACCENT PORCELAIN TILE
W/SMOOTH STUCCO
BENCH

UNIQUE WOOD TRELLIS PANELING NEXT TO THE SHOWER/BENCH LOUNGE AREA

SHOWER

CANTILEVER POOL CABANA W/BAJA LOUNGE & FIRE PIT

WATER CASCADING W/1/2" POOL RETURN LINE

FIRE PIT

BAJA LOUNGE AT CANTILEVER POOL CABANA

BACK TO BACK RAISED DECK W/CASCADING WATERFALL & FIRE PIT

GREEN PARK/HOME CAMPING GROUND

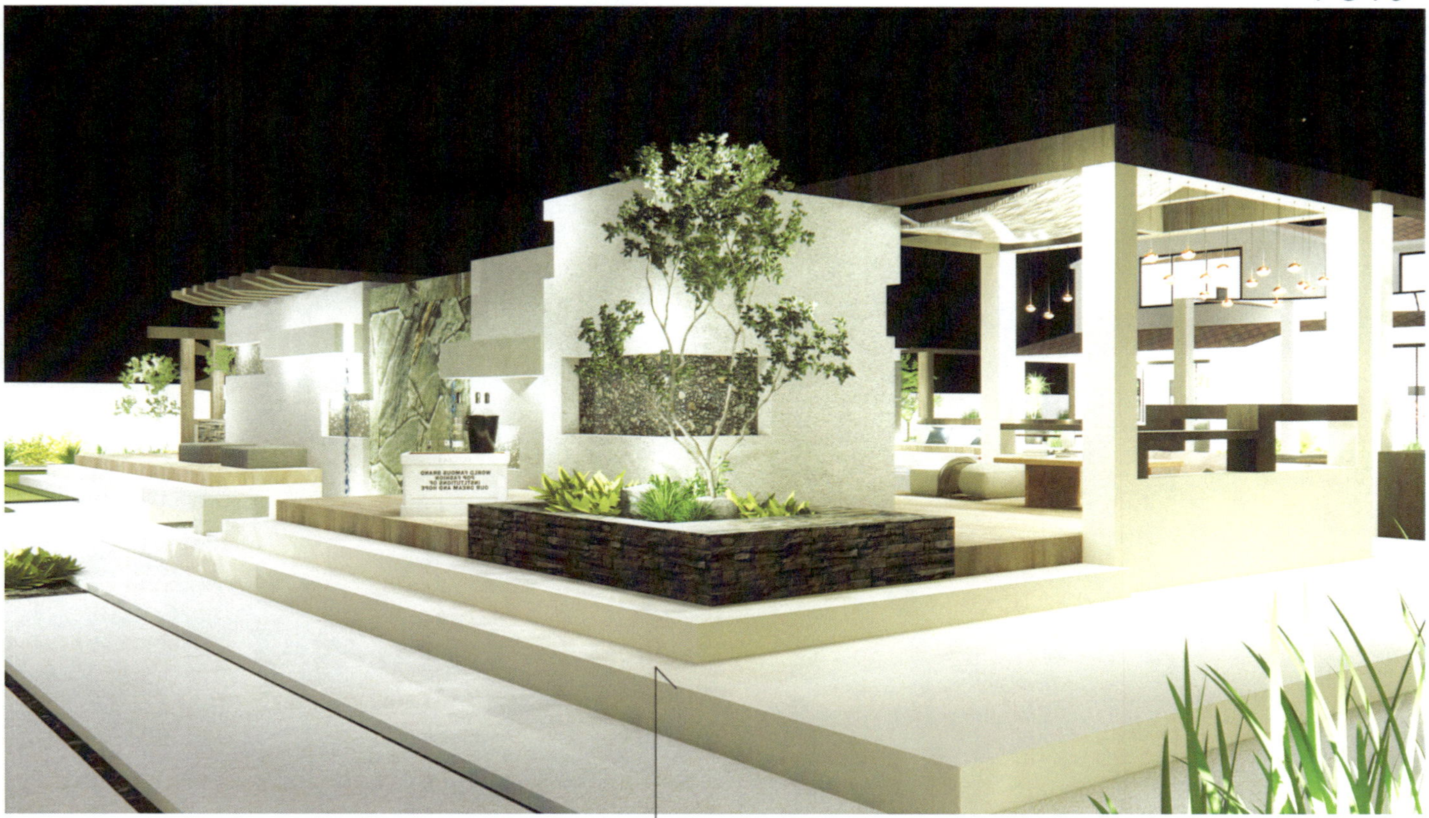

WASHED FINISH COLOR CONCRETE STEPS

BACK TO BACK RAISED DECK LOUNGE VIEWS

(GREEN PARK/HOME CAMPING GROUND SIDE)

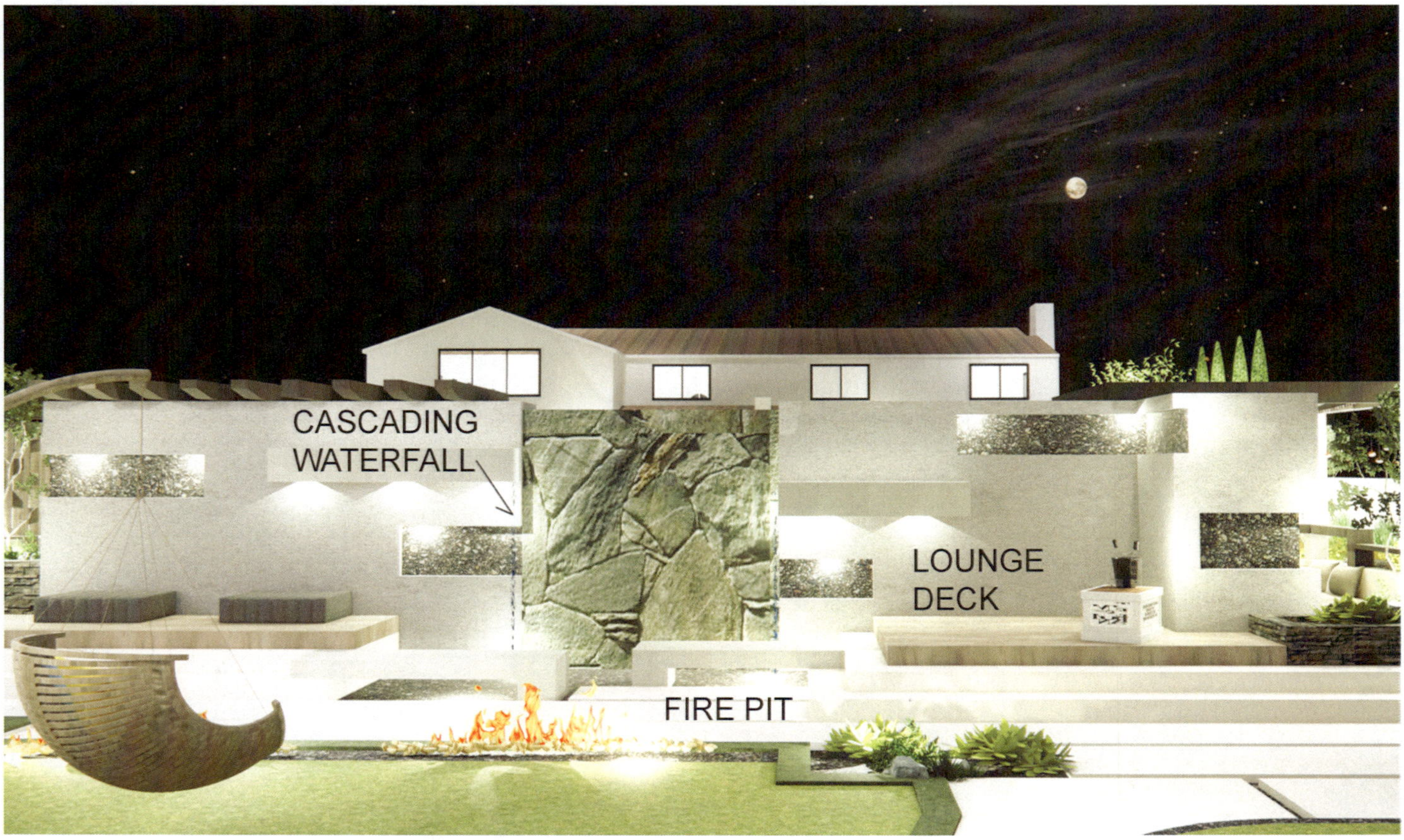

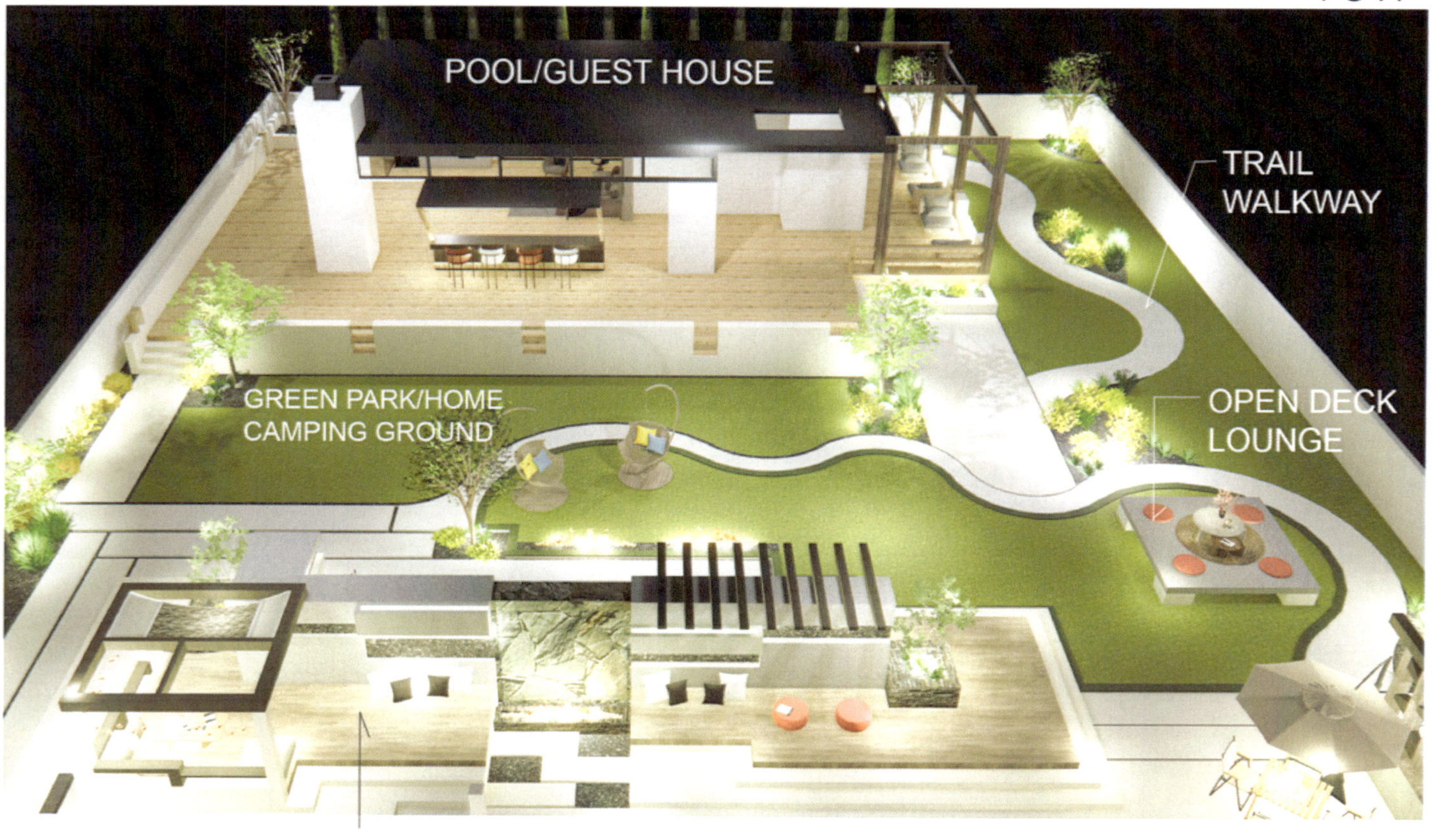

BACK TO BACK RAISED DECK & LOUNGE

BACKYARD POOL/GUEST HOUSE AREA OVER VIEW

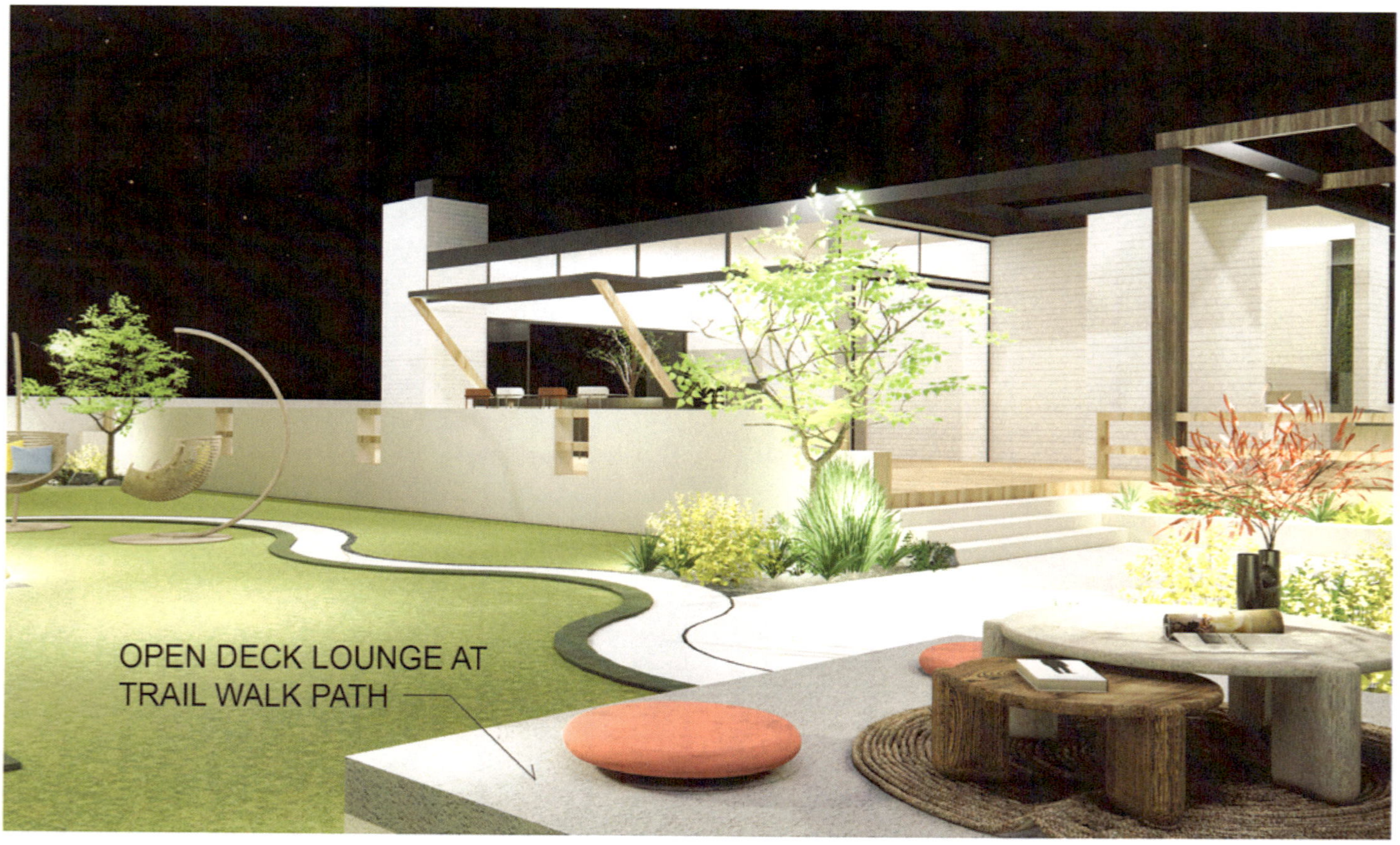

STEP UP

POOL/GUEST
HOUSE PORCH
DECK VIEW

FIRE PIT
AT PORCH
AREA

POOL/GUEST HOUSE OPEN PATIO COVER DECK W/FIRE PIT WALLS

FIXED AWNING ATTACH TO BAR COUNTER

3/4" TEMPER GLASS
SLIDING PANEL WALL

POOL/GUEST HOUSE W/BAR COUNTER

ABOUT THE AUTHOR

Sun Mi Kwon brings over 23 years of experience as a living space and landscape designer, enriched by extensive hands-on expertise. With a robust background in on-site work, she possesses a deep understanding of practical landscape design principles. Throughout her career, Sun Mi has collaborated with a wide spectrum of clients, including private individuals, industry-independent contractors, and architects. Collectively, her contributions have led to the creation of over 1000 unique designs, showcasing her versatility and innovation in the field.

www.ingramcontent.com/pod-product-compliance
Lightning Source LLC
Chambersburg PA
CBRC091242050726
47599CB00009B/961